365 Ways to Calm the Storm Within

*Finding Peace in This
Chaotic World... Every Day*

Jim Lange

ISBN 978-0-9886137-5-1

ISBN 10: 0-9886137-5-1

Cover design by Jennifer Lassiter

Acknowledgements

Thank you to the many people who have supported me in so many ways during the writing of this book.

I want to single out several people who were of tremendous help to me in this project. First, Bill Girrier, Janene Ternes and Susie Joyner for your editing assistance. You each revealed things to me that I had not seen which was extremely valuable to me. Thank you!

I also want to thank David Kaiser for volunteering his services to me in assembling and facilitating the focus groups which proved to be the catalyst to make this project happen.

In addition, thank you for picking up this book. This shows me that you are someone who desires to grow and be a difference-maker. I applaud you for this, because that is rare today. Your growth and increased peace will only help others to grow and become better. So again, thank you!

Most of all, I want to thank God. Thank You Father, I love You!

Introduction

This resource (*365 Ways to the Storm Within: How to Find Peace in this Chaotic World*) came to be for at least two reasons:

1. Because the Lord prompted me to begin producing some resources to help people to find peace in the midst of their chaotic lives and crises;
2. As a result of that prompting, a good friend of mine, David Kaiser, organized a couple of focus groups with people who were in the midst of, or had just come out of, very traumatic circumstances in their lives. The intent was to see where they went, or where they go, for resources to help them find peace when they are in the midst of crises. A common theme began to emerge from these groups...when in the middle of a crisis, many people do not have the energy to read an entire book. Many are just looking for that one quote or saying or principle that they can grasp onto to get through the day.

Since the release of *Calming the Storm Within: How to Find Peace in this Chaotic World* (several years prior to the release of the book you now hold in your hands), I have seen how so many people are craving peace...the type of peace which is not dependent upon life's circumstances.

This book is a great companion to *Calming the Storm Within: How to Find Peace in this Chaotic World* or it can be read as a stand-alone resource.

This book is a bit different in that it contains 365 affirmations, quotes from thought leaders and passages from *Calming the Storm Within*...all designed to help you to discover the peace which surpasses all understanding.

This format should make it easy for you to read one passage a day or several at a time and marinate in the truths and remind yourself of them daily.

If you're like me, you might be tempted to rush through this book to check it off your list (which you could do in little time). However, I believe you will find this much more effective if you take your time in reading through and processing the material presented here. I would suggest setting it next to your computer monitor, or someplace you sit often, and meditating on different points, especially the verses from Scripture. Take time to ponder the truths and ask God to reveal new things to you as you progress through this guide.

And be ready to jot things down which really speak to you.

Regardless of how you utilize this, I hope it blesses you greatly!

Peace be with you!

Jim Lange

Look back over your life. How many "troubles" actually turned out to be great blessings? Do you think God can do that with your current troubles?

Affirmation for today: I can find rest in God amidst my troubles.

My soul finds rest in God alone;
my salvation comes from him.
He alone is my rock and my salvation;
he is my fortress, I will never be shaken.

(Psalm 62:1-2)

"Worrying is carrying tomorrow's load with today's strength - carrying two days at once. It is moving into tomorrow ahead of time. Worrying doesn't empty tomorrow of its sorrow, it empties today of its strength."

~Corrie ten Boom

God IS FAITHFUL! He is a promise keeper!

I can rest in His promises, even in the midst of great difficulty!

"It is well with my soul!"

~Horatio Spafford

Do you remember the great hymn, *It Is Well*? If so, hum it throughout the day. If not, you may want to find it on the internet and let it speak to your soul. Here's the first couple of stanzas:

> When peace, like a river, attendeth my way,
> When sorrows like sea billows roll;
> Whatever my lot, Thou hast taught me to say,
> It is well, it is well with my soul.
>
> It is well with my soul,
> It is well, it is well with my soul.
>
> Though Satan should buffet, though trials should come,
> Let this blest assurance control,
> That Christ hath regarded my helpless estate,
> And hath shed His own blood for my soul.
>
> It is well with my soul,
> It is well, it is well with my soul.

So do not fear, for I am with you;
do not be dismayed, for I am your God.
I will strengthen you and help you;
    I will uphold you with my righteous right hand.
                              (Isaiah 41:10)

"The more you pray, the less you'll panic. The more you worship, the less you worry. You'll feel more patient and less pressured."
                                ~Rick Warren

Axioms to help us prepare for trouble:
1. There is incredible power in prayer;
2. It is very important to be prepared;
3. Our troubles can turn out to be victories when we let God enter in.

Are you a *So Be It Christ-follower*...someone who says, "So be it Lord, I'm following You!" If you are, you will have much more peace in your life.

Do you know what the word "Amen" means? "So be it."

"Whatever is going to happen will happen, whether we worry or not."

~Ana Monnar

Consider it pure joy, my brothers, whenever you face trials of many kinds, because you know that the testing of your faith develops perseverance. Perseverance must finish its work so that you may be mature and complete, not lacking anything.

(James 1:2-4)

Am I seeking to please others or am I seeking to please God alone?

Am I open to receiving peace from God?

"Peace I leave with you; my peace I give you. I do not give to you as the world gives. Do not let your hearts be troubled and do not be afraid."

(The words of Jesus in John 14:27)

"Sorrow looks back, Worry looks around, Faith looks up."

~Ralph Waldo Emerson

"Be still, and know that I am God;
I will be exalted among the nations,
I will be exalted in the earth."
The LORD Almighty is with us;
the God of Jacob is our fortress.   *Selah*

(Psalm 46:10)

Selah means to pause and consider this. Read the above verse again and pause and consider its truth.

Often, serving others is just what is needed to get us out of our "woe is me" rut. Who can you serve today with no expectation of anything in return?

Peace is something provided to us by God (which we need to both seek and receive) that enables us to have tranquility, or be okay on the inside, regardless of our circumstances.

"How can a person deal with anxiety? You might try what one fellow did. He worried so much that he decided to hire someone to do his worrying for him. He found a man who agreed to be his hired worrier for a salary of $200,000 per year. After the man accepted the job, his first question to his boss was, "Where are you going to get $200,000 per year?" To which the man responded, "That's your worry."

~Max Lucado

Seek peace and pursue it.

(Psalm 34:14b)

Am I seeking and pursuing peace from God?

I have been crucified with Christ [in Him I have shared His crucifixion]; it is no longer I who live, but Christ (the Messiah) lives in me; and the life I now live in the body I live by faith in (by adherence to and reliance on and complete trust in) the Son of God, Who loved me and gave Himself up for me.

(Galatians 2:20 AMP)

Dear Lord, please help me understand this thing You have made available to each of us...this thing called "peace." I desperately want more peace, Father, and I thank You for making it so readily available. Help me to seek it out and to go get it, while at the same time receive it from You. I don't want to rely on my circumstances to determine the level of peace in my life. Please help me to be a *So be it* person, someone who is at peace regardless of what is happening in my life. Open my heart to what You have to say to me as I read this book. Thank you
Lord! Amen.

He who dwells in the shelter of the Most High
will rest in the shadow of the Almighty.
I will say of the LORD, "He is my refuge and my
fortress, my God, in whom I trust."

(Psalm 91:1-2)

"I have known many sorrows, most of
which never happened."

~Mark Twain

What are you worrying about? Is there a chance it
won't even happen?

An anxious heart weighs a man down.

(Proverbs 12:25a)

"You cannot find peace by avoiding life."
~Virginia Woolf

"I am the true vine, and my Father is the gardener. He cuts off every branch in me that bears no fruit, while every branch that does bear fruit he prunes so that it will be even more fruitful."
(the words of Jesus in John 15:1-2)

Pruning is painful. However, only a God who loves you would prune you to make you more fruitful. Can you see how this "pruning" can be for your own good?

"Never worry alone. When anxiety grabs my mind, it is self-perpetuating. Worrisome thoughts reproduce faster than rabbits, so one of the most powerful ways to stop the spiral of worry is simply to disclose my worry to a friend... The simple act of reassurance from another human being [becomes] a tool of the Spirit to cast out fear -- because peace and fear are both contagious."

~John Ortberg

Because God loves us, He will continually try to move us out of our comfort zones. It is in this place is where true growth happens so do your best to embrace it.

"Because he loves me," says the LORD, "I will rescue him;
I will protect him, for he acknowledges my name.
He will call upon me, and I will answer him;
I will be with him in trouble,
I will deliver him and honor him.
With long life will I satisfy him
and show him my salvation."

(Psalm 91:14-16)

Affirmation for today: I am forgiven of all my sins and purified from all unrighteousness.

If we confess our sins, he is faithful and just and will forgive us our sins and purify us from all unrighteousness.

(1 John 1:9)

"Therefore I tell you, do not worry about your life, what you will eat or drink; or about your body, what you will wear. Is not life more important than food, and the body more important than clothes? Look at the birds of the air; they do not sow or reap or store away in barns, and yet your heavenly Father feeds them. Are you not much more valuable than they? Who of you by worrying can add a single hour to his life?"

(The words of Jesus in Matthew 6:25-27)

"And why do you worry about clothes? See how the lilies of the field grow. They do not labor or spin. Yet I tell you that not even Solomon in all his splendor was dressed like one of these. If that is how God clothes the grass of the field, which is here today and tomorrow is thrown into the fire, will he not much more clothe you, O you of little faith?"

(The words of Jesus in Matthew 6:28-30)

"So do not worry, saying, 'What shall we eat?' or 'What shall we drink?' or 'What shall we wear?' For the pagans run after all these things, and your heavenly Father knows that you need them. But seek first his kingdom and his righteousness, and all these things will be given to you as well. Therefore do not worry about tomorrow, for tomorrow will worry about itself. Each day has enough trouble of its own."

(The words of Jesus in Matthew 6:31-34)

"We would worry less if we praised more. Thanksgiving is the enemy of discontent and dissatisfaction."

~H.A. Ironside

No discipline seems pleasant at the time, but painful. Later on, however, *it produces a harvest of righteousness and peace for those who have been trained by it.*

(Hebrews 12:11, emphasis added)

Typically when we have to go in for surgery, we understand that it will be painful. However, we usually also know that it will be good for us.

How does this relate to your present struggles?

Cast your cares on the LORD
and he will sustain you;
he will never let the righteous fall.

(Psalm 55:22)

Affirmation for today: Jesus is enough for me.

"My grace is sufficient for you, for my power is made perfect in weakness."
(The words of Jesus in 2 Corinthians 12:9)

Could God be trying to teach you something in this struggle? If so, what might it be?

Here are a few great questions to ask yourself:
· Do I welcome discipline and correction? Or when corrected am I usually defensive?
· Who in my life knows they have an open invitation to correct me when they see I need it?
· Am I asking God regularly to search my heart (see Psalm 139:23) and show me where I need correction?

Do my answers above show that I am one who wants to grow regardless of how painful it might be?

We all desire inner peace. It is because of this desire, whether we have decided to follow Jesus or not, that God allows chaos (pain, turmoil, trouble) in our lives. He knows that the only place to find true peace is through Him. Hopefully, the chaos in our lives draws us closer to Him, where we can find true peace.

Therefore, it is imperative that we learn to embrace the chaos. Know that it is for our good...to help us. Simply knowing this should help us to overcome whatever we encounter, regardless of how chaotic it may be.

Affirmation for today: I am God's child for I am born of the incorruptible seed of the Word of God which lives and abides forever.

For you have been born again, not of perishable seed, but of imperishable, through the living and enduring word of God.

(1 Peter 1:23)

"Worry is most often a prideful way of thinking that you have more control over life and its circumstances than you actually do."

~June Hunt

The LORD is my light and my salvation—
whom shall I fear?
The LORD is the stronghold of my life—
of whom shall I be afraid?

(Psalm 27:1)

Heavenly Father, thank You for loving me so much that You would allow chaos and trouble in my life. You know what I need and You know that staying in my comfort zone is not good for me. Help me to remember this the next time I face chaos and to be thankful in the midst of the storm. Help me to see it from Your vantage point so that I can choose peace in the midst of it and I can be looking for You during the turmoil. Amen.

Cast all your anxiety on him because he cares for you.

(1 Peter 5:7)

What is a practical way you can cast your anxiety on the Lord?

Affirmation for today: I can trust God and do only what He tells me to do and He will take care of the rest.

Trust in the LORD and do good;
dwell in the land and enjoy safe pasture.
Delight yourself in the LORD
and he will give you the desires of your heart.
Commit your way to the LORD;
trust in him and he will do this:
He will make your righteousness shine like the dawn,
    the justice of your cause like the noonday sun.

(Psalm 37:3-6)

Be still before the LORD and wait patiently for him;
do not fret when men succeed in their ways,
when they carry out their wicked schemes.
Refrain from anger and turn from wrath;
do not fret—it leads only to evil.
For evil men will be cut off,
but those who hope in the LORD will inherit the land.

(Psalm 37:7-9)

"We tend to be preoccupied by our problems when we have a heightened sense of vulnerability and a diminished sense of power. Today, see each problem as an invitation to prayer."

~John Ortberg

Chaos is a part of life that cannot be avoided. We need to actually embrace the chaos because God allows it for our own good.

Affirmation for today: I break free from the need to attach myself to accomplishments or people's approval. I do not need to be special in someone else's eyes. I am free from being approval-driven.

"If I had my life to live over, I would perhaps have more actual troubles but I'd have fewer imaginary ones."

~Don Herold

You are not responsible for the happiness of others. You are responsible TO others but not FOR others.

Jesus replied: " 'Love the Lord your God with all your heart and with all your soul and with all your mind.' This is the first and greatest commandment."

(Matthew 22:37-38)

"If you love me, you will obey what I command."
(The words of Jesus in John 14:15)

Just because you were brought up by looking at success based on the "scoreboard of life," that is not the way God views it. Success to Him has to do with how much you love Him and how obedient you are to His commands.

Affirmation for today: I am a new creation.

Therefore, if anyone is in Christ, he is a new creation; the old has gone, the new has come!
(2 Corinthians 5:17)

If the LORD delights in a man's way,
he makes his steps firm;
though he stumble, he will not fall,
for the LORD upholds him with his hand.

(Psalm 37:23-24)

"Worry divides the mind."

~Max Lucado

There is great freedom when you realize that you don't have to control outcomes. We can only do what God has asked us to do. The outcomes are His responsibility.

Is your lack of time really an issue of trying to control your schedule and pack too much into it? Do you have margin built into your schedule to allow for unexpected events?

Am I allowing others to intimidate me?

He alone is my rock and my salvation; he is my fortress, I will not be shaken.

(Psalm 62:6)

Then Peter got down out of the boat, walked on the water and came toward Jesus. But when he saw the wind, he was afraid and, beginning to sink, cried out, "Lord, save me!"

(Matthew 14:29-30)

It wasn't until Peter took his eyes off Jesus that he began to sink. Are your eyes on Jesus or on the "wind" and the "waves" of life? How can you move them back toward Jesus?

Turn from evil and do good;
then you will dwell in the land forever.
For the LORD loves the just
and will not forsake his faithful ones.
They will be protected forever,
but the offspring of the wicked will be cut off;
the righteous will inherit the land
and dwell in it forever.

(Psalm 37:27-29)

"If someone spits on you, does that make you mad?"
"You bet it does!"
"No it doesn't, it just makes you wet. It is your choice to be angry."

How does this exchange relate to your present circumstances?

"Don't lose today by worrying about tomorrow!!!"
~John F. Herbert

Are you choosing to let go of your peace right now? In much the same way as choosing to be angry, you can only lose your peace when you choose to take your eyes off Jesus.

Affirmation for today: This is not happening TO me, it's happening FOR me!

And we know that in all things God works for the good of those who love him, who have been called according to his purpose.

(Romans 8:28)

Divers are taught that when they get caught in seaweed that they need to quickly become calm, otherwise they can die. The same is true in conflict or a crisis.

Lord, help me to remain calm and take a "sacred pause" to come to You! Amen.

"The devil, darkness, and death may swagger and boast, the pangs of life will sting for a while longer, but don't worry; the forces of evil are breathing their last. Not to worry...He's risen!"
~Charles R. Swindoll

Your peace cannot be taken from you without your consent.

Did you realize that everything that "steals" your peace is really a control problem, rooted in fear? Isn't it true that the reason you are fretting is because things are not going your way?

When faced with any situation, we have only two choices:

1. We can attempt to take control to manipulate an outcome or;
2. We can relinquish control and leave the outcome to God.

Trying to control things in order to manage an outcome will always produce stress and anxiety in us. What steps can you take today to relinquish control of the outcomes in your life?

The salvation of the righteous comes from the LORD; he is their stronghold in time of trouble.
The LORD helps them and delivers them;
he delivers them from the wicked and saves them,
because they take refuge in him.

(Psalm 37:39-40)

Affirmation for today: I am delivered from the power of darkness and brought into the Kingdom of Jesus who redeems and forgives me.

For he has rescued us from the dominion of darkness and brought us into the kingdom of the Son he loves, in whom we have redemption, the forgiveness of sins.

(Colossian 1:13-14)

Why are you trying to control things? Is it because of fear?

"Worry is the interest you pay on a debt you may not owe."

~Keith Caserta

When you are trying to control things, aren't you basically telling God that you trust yourself more than Him?

I have been crucified with Christ and I no longer live, but Christ lives in me. The life I live in the body, I live by faith in the Son of God, who loved me and gave himself for me.

(Galatians 2:20)

On the day I called, you answered me; my strength of soul you increased.

(Psalm 138:3 ESV)

To give up your desire to control, you must become dead to yourself. After all, a dead person can't worry or be anxious.

Therefore, I urge you, brothers, in view of God's mercy, to offer your bodies as living sacrifices, holy and pleasing to God—this is your spiritual act of worship.

(Romans 12:1)

"It ain't no use putting up your umbrella till it rains!"

~Alice Caldwell Rice

Shift your thoughts from, "Why is this happening TO me?" to "God, what are You doing FOR me in this?" or "God, what are You trying to teach me here?"

The truth is that God is working on your behalf, even in the midst of the current storm.

Therefore confess your sins to each other and pray for each other so that you may be healed.
(James 5:16a)

Have you been carrying a secret that's getting heavier and heavier? Share it with a trusted friend so that you may be healed. When you do, you will likely find greater peace as well.

"Peace begins with a smile."

~Mother Teresa

"And call upon me in the day of trouble;
I will deliver you, and you will honor me."
(The words of God in Psalm 50:15)

Affirmation for today: I am holy and without blame before Him in love.

For he chose us in him before the creation of the world to be holy and blameless in his sight.
(Ephesians 1:4)

The God of peace will soon crush Satan under your feet.

(Romans 16:20a)

One of the greatest weapons against Satan is your peace.

Let us fix our eyes on Jesus, the author and perfecter of our faith, who for the joy set before him endured the cross, scorning its shame, and sat down at the right hand of the throne of God.

(Hebrews 12:2)

Are your eyes fixed on Jesus or on your problems today?

"Nobody can hurt me without my permission."
~Mahatma Gandhi

Even though I walk
through the valley of the shadow of death,
I will fear no evil,
for you are with me;
your rod and your staff,
they comfort me.

(Psalm 23:4)

"God cannot give us a happiness and peace apart from Himself, because it is not there. There is no such thing."

~C.S. Lewis

Peace isn't stolen from us—we choose to give it up when we refuse to give up control or when we take our eyes off Jesus.

"Thou hast made us for thyself, O Lord, and our heart is restless until it finds its rest in thee."

~Augustine of Hippo

Have you ever considered that God made you for His good pleasure?

Think about some of the worst things you can remember in your life. Now list the good things that you know of that came from that time. Perhaps it is that you were able to help others in a similar spot. Maybe you learned something about yourself. Perhaps you grew from the experience or met someone through it...

God usually looks much better in the rear view mirror than the windshield. He is working right now on your behalf!

Heavenly Father, You are amazing! Thank You for being You, the One in control! Lord, I want peace, the peace that can only come from You. Please forgive me for allowing worry, anxiety and circumstances to steal my peace. I know that this is really a control issue on my part. So please God help me guard my heart and protect me from the enemy and help me let go of those things I want to hang on to. Help me continue to recognize You as the One in control of everything. Amen.

"Grudges are for those who insist that they are owed something; forgiveness, however, is for those who are substantial enough to move on."

~Criss Jami

Affirmation for today: I am strong in the Lord and in His mighty power.

Finally, be strong in the Lord and in his mighty power. (Ephesians 6:10)

On the evening of that first day of the week, when the disciples were together, with the doors locked for fear of the Jews, Jesus came and stood among them and said, "Peace be with you!"(John 20:19)

In this passage, the disciples were locked in a room because of fear. And Jesus appeared and told them, "Peace be with you!" He is telling you that same thing today, "Peace be with you!"

The LORD is good,
a refuge in times of trouble.
He cares for those who trust in him.

(Nahum 1:7)

"You have peace," the old woman said, "when you make it with yourself."

~Mitch Albom

Therefore, since we have been justified through faith, we have peace with God through our Lord Jesus Christ.

(Romans 5:1)

"When Christ died He left a will in which He gave His soul to His Father, His body to Joseph of Arimathea, His clothes to the soldiers, and His mother to John. But to His disciples, who had left all to follow Him, He left not silver or gold, but something far better - His PEACE!"

~Matthew Henry

"Peace is not merely a distant goal that we seek, but a means by which we arrive at the goal."

~Martin Luther King

"I have told you these things, so that in me you may have peace. In this world you will have trouble. But take heart! I have overcome the world."

(The words of Jesus in John 16:33)

Reminders from Jesus:
- In Him you have peace;
- You will have trouble (so don't be surprised by it);
- Regardless of your trouble, Jesus has overcome the world (which includes your trouble)!

The concept of inner peace does not have to be a pipe dream. It is possible and it is something God desires for us...and He has given us a path to follow to peace.

The LORD upholds all those who fall
and lifts up all who are bowed down.

(Psalm 145:14)

"The fruit of Silence is prayer. The fruit of Prayer is faith. The fruit of Faith is love. The fruit of Love is service. The fruit of Service is peace."

~Mother Teresa

Lord God, I am so thankful that You have provided a way to peace. You know my heart Lord, and you know that I desire peace. Please open my eyes to see and my heart to understand. Show me a new way Father. Please don't let me be deceived. I'm counting on You. I'm trusting You. God, lead me. Amen.

Affirmation for today: I am more than a conqueror.

No, in all these things we are more than conquerors through him who loved us.

(Romans 8:37)

Jesus said, "I am the way and the truth and the life. No one comes to the Father except through me."

(John 14:6)

Controversial words, to say the least. Jesus is saying there is only one way. One way to the Father. One way to eternal life. One way to life to the full, including peace. On the surface this sounds awfully exclusive. However, it is actually radically *inclusive* because the door is open to everyone:
- Regardless of your race;
- Regardless of your religious upbringing;
- Regardless of what you have done in your past—
Jesus promises to wipe the slate clean...for real!

The LORD is a refuge for the oppressed,
a stronghold in times of trouble.
Those who know your name will trust in you,
for you, LORD, have never forsaken those who seek you.

(Psalm 9:9-10)

"Develop a pure heart and get to know the Almighty...

- Silence is the secret. It is the first step to be shown His treasures. It is there that you are fully inside yourself and you discover the kingdom which is within.
- Silence your body to listen to the words
- Silence your tongue to listen your thoughts
- Silence your thoughts to listen to your heart beating
- Silence your heart to listen to your spirit
- Silence your spirit to listen to His Spirit

In silence, we leave many to be with the One."

~Mama Maggie Gobran

"No God, no peace. Know God, know peace."
~Unknown

Knowing God truly is the only way to find true and lasting peace. If you do not know God, you can begin the process now. Simply make your own commitment to Him from your heart. Jesus knows your heart, so he'll know if you mean it. It could sound something like this:

> "Jesus, I need help and forgiveness. I can't save myself, only You can. Thank You for dying for me and for being my scapegoat. I want You to be my Lord. I commit from this day forward to serve You, to follow You, to obey You. Please show me the way to do all these things. Amen."

"And I will ask the Father, and he will give you another Counselor to be with you forever—the Spirit of truth."
(The words of Jesus in John 14:15-16a)

How does the thought of the Holy Spirit, the Spirit of truth, being with you forever help you in experiencing peace?

If you have decided to welcome Jesus as your Lord and Savior, congratulations! Angels are rejoicing in heaven (see Luke 15:10) and your name is now written in the Lamb's Book of Life (see Revelation 20:15). You have a new identity. The Holy Spirit now resides inside of you and will give you the desire to glorify God.

In addition, because the Holy Spirit is in you, you have been given the following *fruit* of the spirit, which includes peace:

> But the fruit of the Spirit is love, joy, peace, patience, kindness, goodness, faithfulness, gentleness and self-control.
>
> (Galatians 5:22-23a)

In order for us to truly trust in Jesus, we need to spend time with Him. In John 15, Jesus said, "I am the vine; you are the branches. If a man remains in me and I in him, he will bear much fruit; apart from me you can do nothing."

In other words, hanging out with Jesus will increase the level of peace in your life!

"Peace does not dwell in outward things, but within the soul; we may preserve it in the midst of the bitterest pain, if our will remains firm and submissive. Peace in this life springs from acquiescence to, not in an exemption from, suffering."

~Francois Fenelon

The righteous cry out, and the LORD hears them; he delivers them from all their troubles.

(Psalm 34:17)

"When you pass through the waters, I will be with you; and when you pass through the rivers, they will not sweep over you. When you walk through the fire, you will not be burned; the flames will not set you ablaze. For I am the LORD, your God, the Holy One of Israel, your Savior."

(Isaiah 43:2-3a)

If you have made a recent commitment to the Creator of the Universe then Jesus is your new Lord, your CEO, your Boss. Anytime you get a new boss, you want to find out what he wants you to do, right? No different here. You will want to find out how to walk with Him and follow Him.

Perhaps you know of someone who could help you in this area. If not, ask God for guidance and for Him to bring someone into your life to help guide you.

The LORD gives strength to his people; the LORD blesses his people with peace.

(Psalm 29:11)

The LORD is close to the brokenhearted
and saves those who are crushed in spirit.

(Psalm 34:18)

You were not meant to go on this journey alone. You were meant to travel with others.

Ecclesiastes 4:9-10 says, *Two are better than one, because they have a good return for their work: If one falls down, his friend can help him up. But pity the man who falls and has no one to help him up!*

The fact is that others can help you when you stumble.

They can also challenge you, hold you accountable and help you to grow as Proverbs 27:17 teaches us: *As iron sharpens iron, so one man sharpens another*.

This is extremely important—don't try to do this alone! I encourage you to find a group or at least one person who can help you in this way.

Who is on "your team"?

You were taught, with regard to your former way of life, to *put off your old self*, which is being corrupted by its deceitful desires; to be made new in the attitude of your minds; and to *put on the new self*, created to be like God in true righteousness and holiness.

(Ephesians 4:22-24 emphasis added)

The apostle Paul is telling us that this is not something we are born with. It is something we must do. We must renew our mind. We must **put off** the old self. We must **put on** the new self. It is a choice, not just something that happens.

When you step into your closet, do your clothes just jump on you? Of course not. You need to choose what clothes you are going to wear, then you need to *put them on*. Paul is telling us the same thing. We must *put on* peace and joy. In other words, we must choose to be joyful...always!

How can you change your thinking right now? How can you put on the new self? How can you clothe yourself with peace and joy?

Affirmation for today: I am a joint heir with Christ. (Take some time to ponder the meaning of this)

Now if we are children, then we are heirs—heirs of God and co-heirs with Christ, if indeed we share in his sufferings in order that we may also share in his glory. (Romans 8:17)

"Remember, your worth is founded in Jesus Christ."

~Warren Wiersbe

"You did not choose me, but I chose you and appointed you to go and bear fruit—fruit that will last. Then the Father will give you whatever you ask in my name." (The words of Jesus in John 15:16) Have you asked the Lord, in Jesus' name, for a greater level of peace lately?

"Resign every forbidden joy; restrain every wish that is not referred to God's will; banish all eager desires, all anxiety; desire only the will of God; seek him alone and supremely, and you will find peace."

~Francois Fenelon

Most people want Jesus and the promise of heaven, but they don't want to give up control of their lives. They want to treat Him like they do a breakfast buffet, taking only what they want and leaving the "unappetizing" things. As a result, they miss out on one of the greatest gifts Jesus has for them: a full life, including peace. Much of this desire to control is caused when we dwell on the past or worry about the future.

Are you willing to take ALL of Jesus? Are you willing to give up the life you want for the life Jesus has for you? If you were to do that, what do you think would happen to the level of peace you experience?

I sought the LORD, and he answered me;
he delivered me from all my fears.
Those who look to him are radiant;
their faces are never covered with shame.

(Psalm 34:4-5)

"I have told you these things, so that in me you may have peace. In this world you will have trouble. But take heart! I have overcome the world."

(The words of Jesus in John 16:33)

In the above verse, Jesus did promise trouble...but He didn't ask us to dwell on the upcoming troubles. In fact, in Matthew 6:34, Jesus tells us, "Therefore do not worry about tomorrow, for tomorrow will worry about itself. *Each day has enough trouble of its own*" (emphasis added).

Clearly, Jesus is instructing us to not be worrying about the future.

If we spend too much time in the past, we can be filled with regret. If we spend too much time in the future, we can be filled with worry. Living in the moment allows us to truly set our minds on Jesus rather than our circumstances.

Decide to live in the moment!

"Peace I leave with you; my peace I give you. I do not give to you as the world gives. Do not let your hearts be troubled and do not be afraid."

(The words of Jesus in John 14:27)

Yesterday is history. Tomorrow is a mystery. Today is a gift—that's why they call it the present. I love that statement but I never considered it Biblical until I considered that God refers to Himself as "I Am" throughout the Bible. There is a reason for this, as Helen Mallicoat shares:

I AM

I was regretting the past and fearing the future.
Suddenly my Lord was speaking.
"My name is I AM."
He paused. I waited. He continued,
"When you live in the past with its mistakes and regrets, it is hard. I am not there.
My name is not I WAS.
When you live in the future, with its problems and fears, it is hard. I am not there.
My name is not I WILL BE.
When you live in this moment it is not hard.
I am here,
My name is I AM."

Trust in the LORD with all your heart
and lean not on your own understanding;
in all your ways acknowledge him,
and he will make your paths straight.

(Proverbs 3:5-6)

"Speak, move, act in peace, as if you were in prayer. In truth, this is prayer."

~Francois Fenelon

Affirmation for today: I am complete in Jesus.

For in Christ all the fullness of the Deity lives in bodily form, and you have been given fullness in Christ, who is the head over every power and authority.

(Colossians 2:9-10)

"I have to get to the point of the absolute and unquestionable relationship that takes everything exactly as it comes from Him. God never guides us at some time in the future, but always here and now. Realize that the Lord is here now, and the freedom you receive is immediate."

~Oswald Chambers

God is our refuge and strength, an ever-present help in trouble. Therefore we will not fear, though the earth give way and the mountains fall into the heart of the sea, though its waters roar and foam and the mountains quake with their surging.

(Psalm 46:1-3)

True peace cannot be obtained at a store, through a doctor or from a drug. It can only be received from God. Did you know that of all the adjectives that describe God, He is referred to in Scripture as the "God of peace" more than any other? (Judges 6:24, Isaiah 9:6, Romans 15:33 and 16:20, 1 Corinthians 14:33, Philippians 4:9, 1 Thessalonians 5:23, Hebrews 13:20, Ephesians 2:14)

God is the God of peace. The only way to the God of peace is through His Son, Jesus.

(See John 14:6)

The LORD Almighty is with us;
the God of Jacob is our fortress.

(Psalm 46:7)

Dear God, I am so thrilled and so thankful that You are the God of Peace. Thank you for sending Your Son to die for my sins and to make a way to You. I know that it is only through that sacrifice that peace is possible for me and for that I am so thankful. Lord, help me to live in the moment and help me to have life to the full. Thank you God! Amen.

"We should have much more peace if we would not busy ourselves with the sayings and doings of others."

~Thomas à Kempis

"Remain in me, and I will remain in you. No branch can bear fruit by itself; it must remain in the vine. Neither can you bear fruit unless you remain in me."

(The words of Jesus in John 15:4)

Did you know that peace is one of the nine fruit of the Spirit, along with love, joy and patience?

(see Galatians 5:22-23)

You must remain in Jesus to walk in peace.

Therefore, since we are receiving a kingdom that cannot be shaken, let us be thankful, and so worship God acceptably with reverence and awe, for our "God is a consuming fire."

(Hebrews 12:28-29)

"To fall in love with God is the greatest of all romances; To seek Him, the greatest adventure; To find him, the greatest human achievement."

~Augustine

True peace can only be found through a love relationship with your Heavenly Father.

In all these things we are more than conquerors through him who loved us. (Romans 8:37)

It is only through intimacy with your Heavenly Father that you can experience the peace, which transcends all understanding. You cannot experience the level of peace, which God makes available for you, without knowing Him at a deep level. If you remember nothing else, please hold onto this fact. I implore you to do everything you can to grow in your intimacy with Christ.

Biblical principles are so powerful that they work for everyone, even those who don't believe in Jesus. The truth is, if a non-believer follows Biblical principles, his life will be enhanced. But if you combine the application of the Biblical principles outlined in *Calming the Storm Within* with an intimate relationship with God, you will experience peace that you did not think was possible, the peace which transcends all understanding.

Jesus came and stood among them and said, "Peace be with you!"

(John 20:19b)

"If God be our God, He will give us peace in trouble. When there is a storm without, He will make peace within. The world can create trouble in peace, but God can create peace in trouble."

~Thomas Watson

You can be efficient with your stuff, but if you want to develop a solid relationship, you must be very inefficient in that relationship. This also includes your relationship with God.

But Jesus often withdrew to lonely places and prayed.

(Luke 5:16)

Do you think this was one of the reasons Jesus was at peace? How often do you get alone with God?

I will listen to what God the LORD will say; he promises peace to his people, his saints—but let them not return to folly.

(Psalm 85:8)

"We are not at peace with others because we are not at peace with ourselves, and we are not at peace with ourselves because we are not at peace with God."

~Thomas Merton

I understand, many days you don't feel like spending time with God or you don't feel that you have enough time.

Two truths to ponder:
1. If you let your feelings dictate your actions, you will eventually be in big trouble because our feelings often lie!
2. Everybody has enough time. In fact everyone on the planet has the same amount of time each day, exactly 24 hours.

Affirmation for today: I am alive with Christ.

But because of his great love for us, God, who is rich in mercy, made us alive with Christ even when we were dead in transgressions—it is by grace you have been saved.

(Ephesians 2:4-5)

I will lie down and sleep in peace,
for you alone, O LORD,
make me dwell in safety.

(Psalm 4:8)

"The Christian needs to walk in peace, so no matter what happens they will be able to bear witness to a watching world."

~Henry Blackaby

There are tools that can help*, but there is no 3-step program for seeking God. Check out this incredible promise:

> "You will seek me and find me when you seek me with all your heart. I will be found by you," declares the Lord.
> (Jeremiah 29:13-14a)

The key is a heart which seeks the Lord. However, if you have a heart which seeks God, your actions will follow.

*If you would like some tools to help with developing an intimate relationship with God, go to calmingthestormwithin.com/intimacy

The LORD gives strength to his people;
the LORD blesses his people with peace.
(Psalm 29:11)

As long as I am content to know that He is infinitely greater than I, and that I cannot know Him unless He shows Himself to me, I will have Peace, and He will be near me and in me, and I will rest in Him."

~Thomas Merton

And without faith it is impossible to please God, because anyone who comes to him must believe that he exists and that *he rewards those who earnestly seek him.*

(Hebrews 11:6, emphasis added)

Do you see that? God promises us rewards if we earnestly seek Him. The rewards we are promised are not spelled out, but certainly one of them is peace. Jesus said, "In Me you may have peace" (John 16:33a). So we need to get to know Him to find this peace. The price we must pay is time with Him.

Then the eyes of both of them were opened, and they realized they were naked; so they sewed fig leaves together and made coverings for themselves.

(Genesis 3:7)

Upon sinning, the first thing Adam and Eve did was cover themselves. We do the same thing when we put up our defenses, our walls, our masks. We don't want others to see the "real" us for fear that they might no longer accept or respect us if they really knew us. The strange thing about this is that when someone openly shares with me from a place of vulnerability, I always have a deeper level of respect for him or her.

So believing that keeping things to yourself will help others maintain their respect for you is a lie. In addition, when we become vulnerable we find true healing. I have experienced this personally and I see it repeatedly in the leadership roundtable groups I lead. When people share their true selves, they feel an enormous weight lifted from their shoulders and the healing begins.

Who are the safe people in your life whom you can be real with? Will you commit to be vulnerable with them?

Then the man and his wife heard the sound of the Lord God as he was walking in the garden in the cool of the day, and they hid from the Lord God among the trees of the garden.

(Genesis 3:8)

The second thing Adam and Eve did was to hide from God. When I was in the second grade, I tried to chop down a rather large tree in our front yard with an axe. I was unsuccessful but I did some serious damage to the tree. To top it off, that same day I also threw rocks at our neighbor's brand new car. My mom caught me and said that I would need to explain my escapades to my father. I was in agony that day awaiting my dad's arrival from work, so I hid. Whether or not you have experienced something similar in your life, most of us have, to some extent, done this with God. We often hide from Him, thinking that we are in big trouble and don't want to face the consequences or think that He won't accept us because of our wrongs. No matter the reason, as my dad found me that terrible evening so many years ago, God will find you. He knows everything, even the stuff you try to keep hidden.

Are you real with God? Or are you trying to hide something from Him? You might as well confess it to Him, because He already knows about it anyway.

"See in the meantime that your faith brings forth obedience, and God in due time will cause it to bring forth peace."

~John Owen

Great peace have they who love your law,
and nothing can make them stumble.

(Psalm 119:165)

You will keep in perfect peace
him whose mind is steadfast,
because he trusts in you. Trust in the LORD forever,
for the LORD, the LORD, is the Rock eternal.

(Isaiah 26:3-4)

"Lord, make me an instrument of thy peace. Where there is hatred, let me sow love."

~Francis of Assisi

Affirmation for today: I am free from condemnation.

Therefore, there is now no condemnation for those who are in Christ Jesus, because through Christ Jesus the law of the Spirit of life set me free from the law of sin and death.

(Romans 8:1-2)

LORD, you establish peace for us; all that we have accomplished you have done for us.

(Isaiah 26:12)

There is no use worrying about things over which you have no control, and if you have control, you can do something about them instead of worrying."

~Stanley C. Allen

Would you like to be real with God? I mean really vulnerable and real? If so, it will help you to find greater peace. This is a great prayer to pray regularly:

Search me, O God, and know my heart;
test me and know my anxious thoughts.
See if there is any offensive way in me,
and lead me in the way everlasting.

(Psalm 139:23-24)

And without faith it is impossible to please God, because anyone who comes to him must believe that he exists and that *he rewards those who earnestly seek him.*

(Hebrews 11:6, emphasis added)

Do you see that? God promises us rewards if we earnestly seek Him. The rewards we are promised are not spelled out, but certainly one of them is peace. Jesus said, "In Me you may have peace" (John 16:33a). So we need to get to know Him to find this peace. The price we must pay is time with Him.

"The Christian needs to walk in peace, so no matter what happens they will be able to bear witness to a watching world."

~Henry Blackaby

Do you find yourself in a place where you know it would be good to seek God, but your heart's just not in it? Perhaps the thought of it bores you. Maybe it scares you. Or you're thinking you just don't have enough time for that stuff.

If you are in this place, I have some quick encouragement for you. Seek Him anyway. Admit to God how you feel...after all, you won't be surprising Him with something He doesn't already know.

Ask Him to create in you a heart that desires Him. Even if you don't feel like it, step out in faith believing in God's promises and seek Him until He gives you the desire to spend time with Him.

Do this regularly and I think you will find yourself with a renewed love for God and an increased level of peace in your life:
1. Pray, asking God to increase your desire for Him;
2. In faith, begin spending time with Him and your desire for Him will increase.

Remember, God knows your heart and He promises that if you seek Him with all of it, you will find Him, the God of peace.

(see Jeremiah 29:13-14)

Though the mountains be shaken
and the hills be removed,
yet my unfailing love for you will not be shaken
nor my covenant of peace be removed,"
says the LORD, who has compassion on you.

(Isaiah 54:10)

"Peace comes when there is no cloud between us and God. Peace is the consequence of forgiveness, God's removal of that which obscures His face and so breaks union with Him."

~Charles H. Brent

Intimacy with our Heavenly Father is critical to finding a life filled with peace.

Father God, thank you for Your presence and the way You are making Yourself more and more real in my life. Thank You for Your Son Jesus. I now know that I need Him if I am going to achieve peace, true peace. Jesus, please not only be resident in me, but be my President...the CEO of my life. Change my heart and put in me a desire to want to know You more intimately. I want all of You Lord! Draw me close and help me to trust fully in You! Amen.

"If you love me, you will obey what I command."
(The words of Jesus in John 14:15)

Have you ever considered how your level of obedience relates to your level of love for God? How does your love of God relate to the peace you feel in your life?

Affirmation for today: I am reconciled to God.

All this is from God, who reconciled us to himself through Christ and gave us the ministry of reconciliation.

(2 Corinthians 5:18)

You know the message God sent to the people of Israel, telling the good news of peace through Jesus Christ, who is Lord of all.

(Acts 10:36)

Did you know that God loves you despite the poor choices you've made in your life? There is nothing you can do, or not do, that would make Him love you less.

Do not be anxious about anything, but *in everything, by prayer and petition*, with thanksgiving, present your requests to God. And the peace of God, which transcends all understanding, will guard your hearts and your minds in Christ Jesus.

(Philippians 4:6-7, emphasis added)

Have you ever signed a petition? You know, one of those documents that have a bunch of signatures requesting something. Think about what that represents. In our government, petitions must contain a certain number of valid signatures for the petition to be granted. Paul is telling us here to bring our prayers **and petitions** to God. So if God hasn't answered yet, keep on praying.

Therefore, since we have been justified through faith, we have peace with God through our Lord Jesus Christ, through whom we have gained access by faith into this grace in which we now stand. And we rejoice in the hope of the glory of God.

(Romans 5:1-2)

"As we pour out our bitterness, God pours in his peace."

~F.B. Meyer

I run in the path of your commands, for you have set my heart free.

(Psalm 119:32)

Are you running in the path of God's commands? Can you see how this impacts the level of peace in your life? It is NEVER too late to turn toward God and run in the path of His commands. Why not begin today?

I will walk about in freedom, for I have sought out your precepts. (Psalm 119:45)

When is the last time you sought God through His Word? As this verse says, you can enjoy freedom when you do this.

The mind of sinful man is death, but the mind controlled by the Spirit is life and peace.

(Romans 8:6)

Affirmation for today: I am qualified to share in His inheritance.

Giving thanks to the Father, who has qualified you to share in the inheritance of the saints in the kingdom of light.

(Colossians 1:12)

If your law had not been my delight, I would have perished in my affliction.

(Psalm 119:92)

If you make God's commands, His Word, your delight...it will keep you from perishing even through suffering.

"Self-seeking is the gate by which a soul departs from peace; and total abandonment to the will of God, that by which it returns."

~Madame Guyon

The word righteousness is defined by Merriam-Webster as *acting in accord with divine or moral law : free from guilt or sin*. In other words, righteousness is obeying God. Righteous living will obviously have a positive impact on your circumstances since you won't have as many negative consequences. But is that all God's Word says righteous living is for?

Well, no...

The fruit of righteousness will be peace; the effect of righteousness will be quietness and confidence forever.

(Isaiah 32:17)

Affirmation for today: I am firmly rooted, built up, established in my faith and overflowing with gratitude.

So then, just as you received Christ Jesus as Lord, continue to live in him, rooted and built up in him, strengthened in the faith as you were taught, and overflowing with thankfulness.

(Colossians 2:6-7)

If it is possible, as far as it depends on you, live at peace with everyone. Do not take revenge, my friends, but leave room for God's wrath, for it is written: "It is mine to avenge; I will repay," says the Lord.

(Romans 12:18-19)

In regard to righteousness, you may be thinking, *If the Bible says we all fall short of living righteously (Romans 3:10), it sounds impossible to find this peace that righteousness produces. How can we do this?* That great question has an even greater answer.

This peace is available to us because Jesus has provided the gift of righteousness for all who invite Him to be the Leader of their lives:

For if, by the trespass of the one man, death reigned through that one man, how much more will those who receive God's abundant provision of grace and of the gift of righteousness reign in life through the one man, Jesus Christ.

(Romans 5:17)

"Blessed are the single-hearted, for they shall enjoy much peace... If you refuse to be hurried and pressed, if you stay your soul on God, nothing can keep you from that clearness of spirit which is life and peace. In that stillness you know what His will is."

~Amy Carmichael

Did you know that Jesus' punishment on your behalf actually brings you peace? It's true...because of His great love for you and His desire that you live life to the full...which includes living life with peace.

But he was pierced for our transgressions, he was crushed for our iniquities; *the punishment that brought us peace was upon him*, and by his wounds we are healed.

(Isaiah 53:5, emphasis added)

Living righteously helps us to find peace. We can only live righteously because of the blood Jesus shed on our behalf. Yet, we are to pursue (and even hunger and thirst after) righteousness. Are you doing this?

"Blessed are those who hunger and thirst for righteousness, for they will be filled."

(The words of Jesus in Matthew 5:6)

The LORD detests the way of the wicked but he loves those who pursue righteousness.

(Proverbs 15:9)

For the kingdom of God is not a matter of eating and drinking, but of righteousness, peace and joy in the Holy Spirit, because anyone who serves Christ in this way is pleasing to God and approved by men. Let us therefore make every effort to do what leads to peace and to mutual edification.

(Romans 14:17-19)

Affirmation for today: I am a fellow citizen of the saints and of the household of God.

Consequently, you are no longer foreigners and aliens, but fellow citizens with God's people and members of God's household, built on the foundation of the apostles and prophets, with Christ Jesus himself as the chief cornerstone.

(Ephesians 2:19-20)

The sinners in Zion are *terrified; trembling* grips the godless: "Who of us can dwell with the consuming fire? Who of us can dwell with everlasting burning?"

(Isaiah 33:14, emphasis added)

If we turn away from God and His instructions for us, we will be terrified. When I am driving over the speed limit, my anxiety level is higher because of my fear of being caught. It doesn't have to be this way in our lives.

In addition to fear, disobedience to God brings something else which certainly will detract from peace in our lives, namely the work of Satan:

As for you, you were dead in your transgressions and sins, in which you used to live when you followed the ways of this world and of *the ruler of the kingdom of the air [Satan], the spirit who is now at work in those who are disobedient.*

(Ephesians 2:1-2, emphasis added)

How does your level of obedience to God affect the level of peace in your life?

May the God of hope fill you with all joy and peace as you trust in him, so that you may overflow with hope by the power of the Holy Spirit.

(Romans 15:13)

"Affliction shows the power of Christ's blood, when it gives peace in an hour of trouble, when it can make happy in sickness, poverty, persecution and death. Do not be surprised if you suffer, but glorify God."

~Robert Murray McCheyne

Affirmation for today: I am born of God and the evil one cannot harm me.

We know that anyone born of God does not continue to sin; the one who was born of God keeps him safe, and the evil one cannot harm him.

(1 John 5:18)

In the last half of Matthew, Chapter 6, Jesus addresses the issue of worry. He mentions some things that we often are caught worrying about, clothing, food, etc... He instructs us to not worry about these things, but rather, to "seek first his kingdom and his *righteousness*, and all these things will be given to you as well" (Matthew 6:33 – emphasis added). In other words, if we seek after God's kingdom *and* righteousness, then we won't have to worry at all because He will provide the things for us we were worrying about.

I don't believe this is a one-time thing, though. "Okay, Lord, I just spent a minute seeking righteousness, now gimme!" This has to be a way of life. We must pursue righteousness all the days of our lives.

Great peace have they who love your law, and nothing can make them stumble.
> (Psalm 119:165, emphasis added)

Do you love God's law (His Word)? Ask God to strengthen your love for His Word. It will bring you great peace!

If we willfully disobey God, He will not give us the peace, which transcends all understanding, and we will have to face the natural consequences, which will further hinder our quest for peace.

The God of peace be with you all. Amen.

(Romans 15:33)

"In the secret of God's tabernacle no enemy can find us, and no troubles can reach us. The pride of man and the strife of tongues find no entrance into the pavilion of God. The secret of his presence is a more secure refuge than a thousand Gibraltars. I do not mean that no trials come. They may come in abundance, but they cannot penetrate into the sanctuary of the soul, and we may dwell in perfect peace even in the midst of life's fiercest storms."

~Hannah Whitall Smith

Dear God, You are so Holy. Please examine my heart, Lord, and teach me Your ways. I want to obey You. I want to live a life of righteousness. I now know that the fruit of righteousness is peace. I know that without You and the amazing gift of Jesus' death for me, I cannot be truly righteous and therefore I cannot find true peace. So I thank you for that! I know that I cannot do this alone. I need You God. Please help me. Thank You for Your Word and Your instructions for life. Change my heart and help me desire to know and love You more. Make me a lover of Your Word. Make this a priority in my life so that I can know beyond a shadow of a doubt what obedience looks like. Amen.

Affirmation for today: I am chosen.

For we know, brothers loved by God, that he has chosen you.

(1 Thessalonians 1:4)

There are clearly some things we can do to find an instant level of peace in our lives. However, sustaining that level of peace is impossible on our own. We obviously need help and Jesus is well aware of this. He told his followers that it was for their good (and ours) that He go away because He would send the Counselor to guide them.

(see John 16:7)

To understand the magnitude of this promise, can you imagine walking with Jesus as the disciples did, listening to Him teach each day and witnessing miracle after miracle? It had to be awesome. Yet, Jesus said that it was better that He leave so the Holy Spirit could come. Hard to believe anyone would be better than Jesus, yet Jesus tells us that the Spirit will be of more help to us than Jesus Himself. Amazing.

How does knowing this help you to understand the peace that is available to you?

The God of peace will soon crush Satan under your feet. The grace of our Lord Jesus be with you.

(Romans 16:20)

"If you're missing joy and peace, you're not trusting God."

~Joyce Meyer

It is my belief that most people, including me, do not fully comprehend the incredible power and authority that has been given to us through the Holy Spirit. The Holy Spirit is one of the foundational keys to a life of peace:

> The mind controlled by the Spirit is life and peace.
>
> (Romans 8:6b)

Is your mind controlled by the Holy Spirit?

Grace and peace to you from God our Father and the Lord Jesus Christ.

(1 Corinthians 1:3)

Affirmation for today: I am the apple of my Father's eye and He protects and carries me.

In a desert land he found him,
in a barren and howling waste.
He shielded him and cared for him;
he guarded him as the apple of his eye,
like an eagle that stirs up its nest
and hovers over its young,
that spreads its wings to catch them
and carries them on its pinions.

(Deuteronomy 32:10-11)

Direct me in the path of your commands, for there I find delight.

(Psalm 119:35)

Make this your prayer today and see how this impacts the level of peace in your life.

For God is not a God of disorder but of peace.

(1 Corinthians 14:33)

Being in God's will would certainly help your level of peace. However, many don't know how to be in God's will.

I have a guaranteed way to begin to be in the will of God. Are you ready?

You will begin to move toward God's will if you do one thing: **love God**. That's right, love God.

> One of them, an expert in the law, tested him with this question: "Teacher, which is the greatest commandment in the Law?"
>
> Jesus replied: "'Love the Lord your God with all your heart and with all your soul and with all your mind.' This is the first and greatest commandment."
>
> (Matthew 22:35-38)

Read the above passage again. Jesus is saying that, above everything else, the **most** important thing we can do is love God with all we have. So in God's eyes, loving Him is more important than anything else. It's more important than ministry stuff. It's more important than going to church. It's more important than loving our families.

Am I implying these things are bad? Absolutely not. But God wants our hearts devoted to Him first and foremost, above all that other stuff. If we truly love God with all our heart, we will naturally begin to do these other "good" things...but it will be done from a position of love rather than obligation.

"To win the war against fear, we must know the true God as He is revealed in the Bible. He works to give us lasting peace. He receives joy, not from condemning us but in rescuing us from the devil. Yes, the Lord will bring conviction to our hearts concerning sin, but it is so He can deliver us from sin's power and consequences. In its place, the Lord works to establish healing, forgiveness and peace."

~Francis Frangipane

Affirmation for today: I am being changed unto the Lord's image.

And we, who with unveiled faces all reflect the Lord's glory, are being transformed into his likeness with ever-increasing glory, which comes from the Lord, who is the Spirit.

(2 Corinthians 3:18)

Grace and peace to you from God our Father and the Lord Jesus Christ.

(2 Corinthians 1:2)

Loving God is the first and greatest command-ment for you and for me (see Matthew 22:35-38). This means that it is God's will. If you want to be right in the middle of God's will, you must start here. You cannot bypass this. Loving Him is your No. 1 calling.

Being in God's will is a good place to be. You certainly will have more peace when you are in His will.

Jesus tells us *how* He knows we love Him: "If you love Me, you will obey what I command" (John 14:15). Jesus is saying that if we truly love Him, we will do as He says; we will follow God's plan for our lives. It's that simple...and yet, it can be very difficult.

In Philippians 4:6, we are commanded to not be anxious about anything. These are the words of the Apostle Paul. It's as if he's telling us, "I know you want to be anxious at times; we all do. But trust me, you don't have to go there. Choose not to be anxious. God's got it!" He could also be saying, "If you choose to not be anxious, you are showing your Father how much you love Him!"

Developing an intimate relationship with God brings us to a place of yielding more and more of our lives to the Holy Spirit. As the Holy Spirit works in us at ever-increasing levels, we then desire to obey our Father in all areas of our lives. This in turn leads to an increase in the filling of His Spirit, which brings about a desire for more intimacy with God (see Romans 5:5 and 1 John 4:13), and so on.

"If you love me, you will obey what I command. And I will ask the Father, and he will give you another Counselor to be with you forever—the Spirit of truth."

(The words of Jesus in John 14:15-17a)

But now in Christ Jesus you who once were far away have been brought near through the blood of Christ. For he himself is our peace, who has made the two one and has destroyed the barrier, the dividing wall of hostility, by abolishing in his flesh the law with its commandments and regulations. His purpose was to create in himself one new man out of the two, thus making peace.

(Ephesians 2:13-15)

It is impossible for us to have peace and live the life God has called us to without the help of the Holy Spirit. The Spirit will not do this on His own, but rather will partner with us to bring about this change in our lives.

"If our minds are stayed upon God, His peace will rule the affairs entertained by our minds. If, on the other hand, we allow our minds to dwell on the cares of this world, God's peace will be far from our thoughts."

~Woodrow Kroll

Affirmation for today: Because I have been born of God, I have overcome the world.

For everyone born of God overcomes the world.

(1 John 5:4a)

Father God, thank You for the gift of Your Holy Spirit. I now recognize that in order to have true peace, I must be fully submitted to the Spirit's work in my life. I deeply desire that. Please change my heart, Lord, to one that submits to Your will alone. Continually fill me with Your Spirit. Dear God, please reveal to me my part in this and give me a spirit willing to obey. Amen.

Rejoice in the Lord always. I will say it again: Rejoice!

(Philippians 4:4)

Later in this passage, Paul tells us that if we can rejoice (along with some other things), that the God of peace will be with you.

When does Paul say to rejoice in the Lord? How do you think he could say that (by the way, he wrote this while in prison)?

In order to fully grasp this, we must first understand the difference between joy and happiness. Happiness is an emotion based on circumstances while joy is a quality derived from God Himself. Because of this, it *is* possible to be joyful even when things aren't going well.

For God was pleased to have all his fullness dwell in him [Jesus], and through him to reconcile to himself all things, whether things on earth or things in heaven, by making peace through his blood, shed on the cross. Once you were alienated from God and were enemies in your minds because of your evil behavior. But now he has reconciled you by Christ's physical body through death to present you holy in his sight, without blemish and free from accusation.

(Colossians 1:19-22)

Affirmation for today: I have everlasting life and will not be condemned.

"I tell you the truth, whoever hears my word and believes him who sent me has eternal life and will not be condemned; he has crossed over from death to life."

(The words of Jesus in John 5:24)

"Because of the empty tomb, we have peace. Because of His resurrection, we can have peace during even the most troubling of times because we know He is in control of all that happens in the world."

~Paul Chappell

"One joy shatters a hundred griefs."

~Chinese Proverb

What can you do to cultivate one joy in your life today?

Do not conform any longer to the pattern of this world, but *be transformed by the renewing of your mind.* Then you will be able to test and approve what God's will is—his good, pleasing and perfect will.

(Romans 12:2, emphasis added)

How's your thinking? Have you taken out your head trash lately? This leads to transformation and greater peace.

Now may the Lord of peace himself give you peace at all times and in every way. The Lord be with all of you.

(2 Thessalonians 3:16)

"A great many people are trying to make peace, but that has already been done. God has not left it for us to do; all we have to do is to enter into it."

~D.L. Moody

Being joyful is a choice. Of course, true joy is only possible because of Jesus' joy. The joy He provides is available for us even during tough times if we remain (or abide) in Jesus, if His words remain in us, if we obey His commands and remain in His love:

> "I am the vine; you are the branches. If a man remains in me and I in him, he will bear much fruit; apart from me you can do nothing. If anyone does not remain in me, he is like a branch that is thrown away and withers; such branches are picked up, thrown into the fire and burned. If you remain in me and my words remain in you, ask whatever you wish, and it will be given you. This is to my Father's glory, that you bear much fruit, showing yourselves to be my disciples. "As the Father has loved me, so have I loved you. Now remain in my love. If you obey my commands, you will remain in my love, just as I have obeyed my Father's commands and remain in his love. *I have told you this so that my joy may be in you and that your joy may be complete.*"
>
> (The words of Jesus in John 15:5-11, emphasis added)

Affirmation for today: I can do all things through Christ Jesus.

I can do everything through him who gives me strength.

(Philippians 4:13)

And we know that in all things God works for the good of those who love him, who have been called according to his purpose.

(Romans 8:28)

Remember, God is working on your behalf. In ALL things, He is working FOR you!

"He will easily be content and at peace, whose conscience is pure."

~Thomas à Kempis

Being joyful can help you to discover more peace in your life. With that in mind, consider this:

Be joyful always; pray continually; give thanks in all circumstances, for this is God's will for you in Christ Jesus.

(1 Thessalonians 5:16-18, emphasis added)

As you can see, being joyful is an important aspect of being in God's will. Being in God's will certainly is a more peaceful place.

"Fear not, for I have redeemed you;
I have summoned you by name; you are mine.
When you pass through the waters,
I will be with you;
and when you pass through the rivers,
they will not sweep over you.
When you walk through the fire,
you will not be burned;
the flames will not set you ablaze.

(The words of the Lord in Isaiah 43:1-2)

God, You are the author of all good things. Thank You for joy. I want more joy in my life Lord, so please help me renew my mind so that I may be transformed. Help me rejoice in You always. Help me to choose You over the worries of this life so that Your Word will be able to grow in me and I may be fruitful.
Amen.

Affirmation for today: I press on toward the goal to win the prize of the High calling of God.

I press on toward the goal to win the prize for which God has called me heavenward in Christ Jesus.

(Philippians 3:14)

"Great thoughts of your sin alone will drive you to despair; but great thoughts of Christ will pilot you into the haven of peace."

~Charles Spurgeon

Let your gentleness be evident to all. The Lord is near.

(Philippians 4:5)

Did you know that fostering a spirit of gentleness will make you more peaceful? It's true, read Philippians 4:4-9.

"Only the weak are cruel. Gentleness can only be expected from the strong."

~Leo F. Buscaglia

I have heard it said that it is good to live with convictions yet be easy to get along with. This is gentleness. In other words, it's okay to agree to disagree. It *is* possible to remain friends with those who disagree with you...really.

How are you at being gentle?

After this, the word of the LORD came to Abram in a vision:
"Do not be afraid, Abram.
I am your shield,
your very great reward."

(Genesis 15:1)

Commit your way to the Lord [roll and repose each care of your load on Him]; trust (lean on, rely on, and be confident) also in Him and He will bring it to pass. (Psalm 37:6 AMP)

Have you ever sat on the ground and rolled a ball to a young child? Read the verse above again...and think of rolling your cares to God. Unlike a child, He will not roll it back...your cares are for Him to deal with.

"Prayer girds human weakness with divine strength, turns human folly into heavenly wisdom, and gives to troubled mortals the peace of God. We know not what prayer can do."

~Charles Spurgeon

"Have I not commanded you? Be strong and courageous. Do not be terrified; do not be discouraged, for the LORD your God will be with you wherever you go." (Joshua 1:9)

From my perspective, Churchgoers as a whole have not been gentle with each other. There are constant disagreements between Christians over whose way is the right way. Some people refuse to associate with those who believe in the practice of speaking in tongues or those who baptize infants or use drums and electric guitars during worship or allow jeans in church. I mean, really? How can these attitudes ever bring inner peace? Can't we agree that we worship the same God, that Jesus is our Savior, that the Bible is the inspired Word of God and agree to disagree on the other stuff?

If you think you just don't have that "considerate" or "gentleness" gene and this is something that seems impossible for you, don't believe it. Just as peace is one of the fruit of the Spirit, so too is gentleness (see Galatians 5:22-23). So, it is already in us if we are a believer in Christ. If you are feeling the opposite of being gentle, ask the Holy Spirit to help you to develop the fruit of gentleness.

Affirmation for today: Greater is He who is in me than he who is in the world.

You, dear children, are from God and have overcome them, because the one who is in you is greater than the one who is in the world.

(1 John 4:4)

Then you will have success if you are careful to observe the decrees and laws that the LORD gave Moses for Israel. Be strong and courageous. Do not be afraid or discouraged.

(1 Chronicles 22:13)

"There cannot be any peace where there is uncertainty."

~Charles Spurgeon

Pride goes before destruction, a haughty spirit before a fall.

(Proverbs 16:18)

Being prideful is one way to not be gentle. The fall that is sure to come with pride will probably also not be very peaceful.

Think about your peace stealers, or rather the things which you allow to take your peace. Every peace stealer involves your desire to control the situation. Well, that control is our selfish desire. We want it a certain way and when it doesn't work out that way, we let go of our peace.

What are you trying to control right now? How would letting go of that control help increase your peace?

If God is for us, who can be against us?

(Romans 8:31b)

Affirmation for today: I always triumph in Christ.

But thanks be to God, who always leads us in triumphal procession in Christ and through us spreads everywhere the fragrance of the knowledge of him.

(2 Corinthians 2:14)

"We cannot enjoy peace in this world unless we are ready to yield to the will of God in respect of death. Our times are in His hand, at His sovereign disposal. We must accept that as best."

~John Owen

Being gentle and considerate brings great power and allows us to think more of others than ourselves, which brings peace.

Abba Father, thank You for giving us such a great example of gentleness in Jesus. Lord, I want to become meeker and gentler, like Jesus. Help me be less demanding. Help me think of others more often and of myself less often. God, remove my selfish ways! Thank You Lord! Amen.

"Do not be afraid of those who kill the body but cannot kill the soul. Rather, be afraid of the One who can destroy both soul and body in hell."
(The words of Jesus in Matthew 10:28)

Are you more eager to please God or others?

Consider it pure joy, my brothers, whenever you face trials of many kinds, because you know that the testing of your faith develops perseverance. Perseverance must finish its work so that you may be mature and complete, not lacking anything.

(James 1:2-4)

Can you see how your present trials are helping you to grow and develop?

Do not be anxious about anything, but in everything, by prayer and petition, with thanksgiving, present your requests to God.

(Philippians 4:6, emphasis added)

Did you know that, with the help of the Holy Spirit, you can *choose* to not be anxious? This is truth.

"Don't let tomorrow take up too much of today!"
~Kristin Lange
(a sign hanging in my office,
made by my daughter)

We must accept finite disappointment, but we must never lose infinite hope.
~Martin Luther King

Affirmation for today: I am Jesus' friend because I do what He commands.

"You are my friends if you do what I command. I no longer call you servants, because a servant does not know his master's business. Instead, I have called you friends, for everything that I learned from my Father I have made known to you."

(The words of Jesus in John 15:14-15)

In my anguish I cried to the LORD,
and he answered by setting me free.
The LORD is with me; I will not be afraid.
What can man do to me?
The LORD is with me; he is my helper.
I will look in triumph on my enemies.
It is better to take refuge in the LORD
than to trust in man.
It is better to take refuge in the LORD
than to trust in princes.

(Psalm 118:5-9)

Young men, in the same way be submissive to those who are older. All of you, *clothe yourselves* with humility toward one another, because, "God opposes the proud but gives grace to the humble."
(1 Peter 5:5, emphasis added)

God is all powerful, but He wants to partner with us in our growth. How would *clothing* yourself with humility help you to be more peaceful?

From a simplistic point of view, self-control boils down to a choice. Every time you have a choice to make, you ask a question of yourself, whether you're consciously aware of it or not. That question is, *Am I going to do what I want to do or am I going to do my best to honor God?*

How would consistently asking this question when you have choices to make help you to be more peaceful?

O house of Israel, trust in the LORD—
he is their help and shield.
O house of Aaron, trust in the LORD—
he is their help and shield.
You who fear him, trust in the LORD—
he is their help and shield.

(Psalm 115:9-11)

Do not be anxious about anything.

(Philippians 4:6a)

If he wanted to be a bit more direct with us, Paul (the author of the above verse) might say, "Listen. When you are anxious, you are basically telling God that you don't trust Him to handle this. So do you trust God or not?"

Ultimately, isn't that the bottom-line when it comes to anxiety? When I'm anxious, I'm showing God by my behavior that I am going to handle this, I don't need Him and I certainly don't believe He can help me. That may be one of the most prideful things I can do and that's not good. (*God opposes the proud but gives grace to the humble.* 1 Peter 5:5) In this case, I am sinning.

Affirmation for today: I have been bought at a great price...I belong to God.

Do you not know that your body is a temple of the Holy Spirit, who is in you, whom you have received from God? You are not your own; you were bought at a price. Therefore honor God with your body.

(1 Corinthians 6:19-20)

If you are lacking self-control like I am in certain areas of my life, I would suggest asking God regularly to increase your self-control. You might even ask Him to give you opportunities to exercise it. (Be careful. This could be challenging, as He might allow more temptation to be brought to you.) I would also suggest asking God to bring people into your life who can hold you accountable in these areas.

Who's on your team or inner circle who you can ask to hold you accountable? This will help to bring a greater level of peace into your life.

Be strong and courageous. Do not be afraid or terrified because of them, for the LORD your God goes with you; he will never leave you nor forsake you."

(Deuteronomy 31:6)

"Problems are not stop signs, they are guidelines."

~Robert Schuller

My soul finds rest in God alone;
my salvation comes from him.
He alone is my rock and my salvation;
he is my fortress, I will never be shaken.

(Psalm 62:1-2)

Make this verse into a song and sing this to yourself today—you can use something like this:

You are my Rock,
You're my Salvation;
You are my Fortress,
I will never be shaken.

"I have told you these things, so that in me you may have peace. In this world you will have trouble. But take heart! I have overcome the world."

(The words of Jesus in John 16:33)

Our lives are so unpredictable. One of the few constants in life is change. Jobs are lost. Health falters. Loved ones pass away. Relationships get rocky. Stress comes like a tidal wave. Our comfort zones get snatched away. Remember: Jesus promised us trouble (see above verse). We ALL will face it.

Read the above verse again. What else does Jesus promise?

Affirmation for today: I am a citizen of Heaven.

But our citizenship is in heaven. And we eagerly await a Savior from there, the Lord Jesus Christ.
(Philippians 3:20)

Jesus said, "Do not let your hearts be troubled. Trust in God; trust also in me"

(John 14:1).

Jesus is telling us, "Just jump in, you can trust Me, I'll catch you."

When I am afraid,
I will trust in you.
In God, whose word I praise,
in God I trust; I will not be afraid.
What can mortal man do to me?

(Psalm 56:3-4)

Did you know that when you worry, it dishonors God? Your worry is effectively saying that God is not big enough to handle it, or that you trust yourself more than you trust God.

Affirmation for today: God IS FAITHFUL! He is a promise keeper!

I can rest in His promises, even in the midst of opposition. I no longer need to doubt! And, I will expect opposition from others so I must be ready!

For I am the Lord, your God,
who takes hold of your right hand
and says to you, Do not fear;
I will help you.

(Isaiah 41:13)

Here is a good question to ask yourself regularly: *Is God all stressed out about this situation?* Is He saying, "Oh My Self, what am I going to do?" If the answer to either of those questions is "No," don't you think He wants us to chill out too?

We must choose to not be anxious!

"Our vision is so limited we can hardly imagine a love that does not show itself in protection from suffering.... The love of God did not protect His own Son.... He will not necessarily protect us – not from anything it takes to make us like His Son. A lot of hammering and chiseling and purifying by fire will have to go into the process."

~Elisabeth Elliot

If you are a Christian, you know that you will spend eternity in Heaven after your life here on earth. We know that eternity is far, far greater than one million years – in fact, it will *never* end. Our earthly life is still but a drop in the bucket compared to eternity. Our problems, our issues, the things that get us all tied up in knots and keep us up at night are but the smallest of blips on the radar compared with eternity.

God promises us that in **all** things, He works for the good of those who love Him and are called according to His purpose (see Romans 8:28). He doesn't say in the *good* things or in *some* things or even *most* things. He says in ALL things.

Do you believe this? If you truly did, what would happen to your level of peace?

You can't rely on your feelings and emotions. The only thing you can rely on is God and His word.

Your feelings fib and your emotions lie when they don't comply with the word of God.

"Battles are fought in our minds every day. When we begin to feel the battle is just too difficult and want to give up, we must choose to resist negative thoughts and be determined to rise above our problems. We must decide that we're not going to quit. When we're bombarded with doubts and fears, we must take a stand and say: 'I'll never give up! God's on my side. He loves me, and He's helping me! I'm going to make it!*"

~Joyce Meyer

God wants us talking with Him about everything. When we do this, it brings us peace.

Consider a man lost in the desert who was near death for lack of water. He came across a pump with a note and a canteen hung on the handle. The note read: "Below you is all the fresh water you could ever need, and the canteen contains exactly enough water to prime the pump."

For a lot of us, it would be difficult to believe the promise contained in the note. It would be hard for me to empty the entire contents of the canteen into the pump for the promise of unlimited water. Such an act would require tremendous faith. What if it were a lie? I could die of thirst.

This is a great picture of the choice we have when anxiety is facing us. We can choose to drink the water that is visible (in other words, try to deal with it on our own and be anxious) or, we can elect to exercise our faith and pour that water into the well to prime the pump which can produce much, much more water (choose to trust God, which will bring peace).

Lord God, thank You for being so perfect! Father, I don't want to be anxious anymore. Please help me to simply choose not to be anxious from this point forward. Help me "prime the pump" and increase my faith in You. Help me see the big picture and understand that from an eternal perspective, my problems are so insignificant. Bring others into my life to help me keep my focus on You and to help me in the area of self-control. Help me remember that we truly have already won! Remind me often of Your promise that You will never leave me nor forsake me. Lord, I choose peace instead of anxiety and worry! Amen.

Do not be anxious about anything, but *in everything, by prayer and petition*, with thanksgiving, present your requests to God. And the peace of God, which transcends all understanding, will guard your hearts and your minds in Christ Jesus.

(Philippians 4:6-7, emphasis added)

How might praying help you with your current troubles and help you to find greater peace?

Be on your guard; stand firm in the faith; be men of courage; be strong.

(1 Corinthians 16:13)

"To be a Christian without prayer is no more possible than to be alive without breathing."

~Martin Luther King, Jr.

How is your prayer life? What impact does that have on your current level of peace?

Affirmation for today: God is allowing this difficulty FOR my benefit!

Lord, will you please show me what You are trying to teach me through this and what You are doing on my behalf in this?

"I would go to the deeps a hundred times to cheer a downcast spirit. It is good for me to have been afflicted, that I might know how to speak a word in season to one that is weary."

~Charles Spurgeon

"And I will do whatever you ask in my name, so that the Son may bring glory to the Father. You may ask me for anything in my name, and I will do it."

(The words of Jesus in John 14:13-14)

Have you asked Jesus for greater peace?

If you are in the midst of asking God for something that is not being fulfilled now, take heart—God knows what He is doing. He truly has your best interests at heart and will give you only what He sees as appropriate for the time.

If you can truly trust in this fact, that God cares deeply for you in *every* area of your life, that He truly wants you coming to Him in prayer for *everything*...even the silly things, going to Him in prayer will help you experience the peace of God which transcends all understanding.

In praying for something, even if your request is not granted, you can trust that God knows what is best and that He will handle your anxiety about it. The simple act of going to Him in prayer is like a trade: He will take your anxiety and trade it for peace if you let Him. 1 Peter 5:7 says this: *Cast all your anxiety on him because he cares for you.*

Do not be anxious about anything, but *in everything*, by prayer and petition, *with thanksgiving*, present your requests to God. And the peace of God, which transcends all understanding, will guard your hearts and your minds in Christ Jesus.

(Philippians 4:6-7, emphasis added)

What would you say your thanksgiving quotient is? Are you currently thankful, even for your troubles? How might this help you to find more peace?

"God knows our situation; He will not judge us as if we had no difficulties to overcome. What matters is the sincerity and perseverance of our will to overcome them."

~C.S. Lewis

Affirmation for today: I am a success regardless of how I feel right now!

I'm a success simply because God loves me greatly and I love Him and others.

"'Our Father in heaven,
hallowed be your name,
your kingdom come,
your will be done
on earth as it is in heaven.
Give us today our daily bread.
Forgive us our debts,
as we also have forgiven our debtors.
And lead us not into temptation,
but deliver us from the evil one.'"
(The Lord's Prayer, Matthew 6:9b-13)

Have you ever felt too intimidated to pray? If you look at the Lord's Prayer above, you might notice something: it is relatively short. It is five verses long. Ten lines. Four sentences. Fifty-two words.

That's it. Nothing real fancy. No "Christian-eze." Just ordinary words spoken to an extraordinary God. You don't need to speak fancy words at all. Check out these instructions from Jesus in Matthew 6:5-8:

"And when you pray, do not be like the hypocrites, for they love to pray standing in the synagogues and on the street corners to be seen by men. I tell you the truth, they have received their reward in full. But when you pray, go into your room, close the door and pray to your Father, who is unseen. Then your Father, who sees what is done in secret, will reward you. And when you pray, do not keep on babbling like pagans, for they think they will be heard because of their many words. Do not be like them, for your Father knows what you need before you ask him."

Keep your lives free from the love of money and be content with what you have, because God has said,
       "Never will I leave you;
       never will I forsake you."
       So we say with confidence,
       "The Lord is my helper; I will not be afraid.
       What can man do to me?"
                    (Hebrews 13:5-6)

Did you know that you don't need to pray eloquent, long prayers. God just wants you to have a normal conversation with Him. He wants you to share everything with Him, even the tough stuff, even the stuff that seems trivial. He wants you to keep it simple. Why not begin sharing with God what's on your mind right now?

Jesus replied, "I tell you the truth, if you have faith and do not doubt, not only can you do what was done to the fig tree, but also you can say to this mountain, 'Go, throw yourself into the sea,' and it will be done. If you believe, you will receive whatever you ask for in prayer."

(Matthew 21:21-22)

If you ask God for more peace, do you believe He'd give it to you?

Do not be anxious about anything, *but in everything*, by prayer and petition, with thanksgiving, present your requests to God. And the peace of God, which transcends all understanding, will guard your hearts and your minds in Christ Jesus.

(Philippians 4:6-7, emphasis added)

Look at the word that is highlighted: "everything." I love this because it is an open invitation to bring everything to our Father, even the whereabouts of that one sock that always seems to be missing when the laundry is finished. "Lord, please help me to find my missing sock," is a prayer that I believe would please God and make Him smile.

Is there anything which you are allowing to steal your peace that you haven't gone to Him about?

Affirmation for today: I am the son/daughter of the King of kings! I am royalty regardless of my circumstances!

On his robe and on his thigh he has this name written: KING OF KINGS AND LORD OF LORDS.

(Revelation 19:16)

You are all sons of God through faith in Christ Jesus.

(Colossians 3:26)

"Nothing but encouragement can come to us as we dwell upon the faithful dealing of our Heavenly Father in centuries gone by. Faith in God has not saved people from hardships and trials, but it has enabled them to bear tribulations courageously and to emerge victoriously."

~Lee Robertson

As a parent, when your toddler is playing with her play kitchen and she comes to you and asks you with that serious face, "Mommy, can you help me make pisgetti?" you can't help but smile, right? And don't you feel honored that they feel so connected with you that they would ask you to help them with this "imaginary" task?

Okay, I know that your first reaction might be, "Can't you see that I'm busy making real pisgetti?" But if you stopped to think about it, it is pretty cool that they come to you. Well, that is how God is with us...He loves to be with us in **everything**, even our imaginary pisgetti.

Affirmation for today: I will be responsible TO others but I cannot be responsible FOR them. I can only be responsible FOR me and I can be respectful to others.

I believe prayer is one of the things God has shown us that brings peace, because prayer is really nothing more than bringing what's on our mind to God. Even the stuff that is causing us to let go of our peace.

Have you ever shared a secret with someone - something that's been burdening you? Chances are that you felt great relief in getting this off your chest, as if the weight of the world had been lifted off your shoulders.

God desperately wants us to get real with Him and share with Him. He wants to carry our burdens, no matter how big they are. He wants to lighten our load. He wants to bring us peace. Besides, He already knows all our secrets, so we might as well be real with Him.

Get real with God...even right now and see how this helps your level of peace.

I look at prayer as faith in action. Yes, I can pray about something, but will I really believe it? Will my actions show that I believe God has it covered?

The litmus test for me usually revolves around my desire to take control of the issue. I want to wrestle with it until I get an answer. I feel like if I'm not in there "fighting the fight" I certainly won't be able to figure this thing out. If I'm not worrying about it, nothing's going to happen. What a lie. Worrying and fretting are one of the worst things we do because we are basically saying to God, "I don't believe You can handle this." Can there be anything more offensive to tell the King of Kings?

If my faith in God is strong, I will view this differently. I will say, "God, this is bigger than I can figure out. Can you take care of this for me? I'm going to lay this down at Your feet and trust that You're going to handle it." And, I will believe that He will and I won't rush to pick it back up. This is where peace comes—when I know that my Daddy's going take care of it one way or another.

Can you relate to this? If so, what can you do to relinquish control to God?

When we are faced with something that is anxiety producing, we really have two choices: we can choose to fret about it or we can choose to give it to God in prayer. Fretting is really a choice of pride. "I don't need anyone to help with this. I've got it covered." Isn't that what you're saying when you try to "go it alone?" Sure it is. It is telling God that you don't need Him. That is pride with a capital *P*.

I have heard it said that fretting magnifies the problem but prayer magnifies God. Very true.

Rejoice in the Lord always. I will say it again: Rejoice!

(Philippians 4:4)

You can choose to be joyful in all circumstances and this will help you to experience peace.

Affirmation for today: When others initiate conflict with me, it is usually because of something going on inside of them.

Lord, please reveal if there is any truth in what was said about me. Then help me to discard the rest.

You do not have, because you do not ask God. When you ask, you do not receive, because you ask with wrong motives.

(James 4:2b-3a)

Is there something you have not asked for that might help you to be more at peace? Have you checked your motives?

"The ultimate measure of a man is not where he stands in moments of comfort, but where he stands at times of challenge and controversy."
~Martin Luther King, Jr.

Father, You are so awesome. I am so thankful that You have made a way for me to communicate directly with You! Please Lord, help me do so more often! Help me to love prayer and hate sin. Help me to be thinking about You all the time so that I can come to You about anything, anytime. Help me to pray persistently and expectantly. And please reveal to me anything that might be hindering my prayers. Amen.

Finally, brothers, whatever is true, whatever is noble, whatever is right, whatever is pure, whatever is lovely, whatever is admirable—if anything is excellent or praiseworthy—think about such things.

(Philippians 4:8)

What are you focusing on? How will focusing on the above things help you in your quest for peace?

Affirmation for today: I cannot make someone else happy.

I can trust that their happiness is God's problem not mine. All I can do is seek God with all my heart and be the best me I can be.

If someone is angry at me, it is likely more of an indication of something going on in them than something going on in me.

"Instead of complaining that the rosebush is full of thorns, be happy that the thorn bush has roses."

~German Proverb

How can this German proverb be applied to your life right now?

Trust in him at all times, O people;
pour out your hearts to him,
for God is our refuge.

(Psalm 62:8)

"I will love the light for it shows me the way, yet I will endure the darkness for it shows me the stars."

~Og Mandino

When things are tough in your life, who are you thinking about most of the time? Be honest now. It's *you,* right? Sure it is. If I'm honest, even when things are going *well,* I'm thinking about *me* most of the time. Ever since Adam and Eve brought sin into the world, we human beings have been a selfish lot. We are born that way.

So what does this have to do with peace? I have seen that when I (or others I know) wallow in self pity and only think about myself, I can get to a place of depression or at least feeling down about things. Yet, when I have been able to break through that feeling and focus on someone else and how I might help them, it does something in my mind and in my heart. I have a renewed bounce in my step. I have purpose. I have more peace. Perhaps it is because I simply have taken my mind off my issues and me. Or perhaps, it is because I am doing what God wants me to do and I am getting away from that *stinkin' thinkin',* which includes thinking only about me.

Intimacy with Jesus is of paramount importance and is the most important thing you can develop to help you find the peace which transcends all understanding.

The only way to abide, or develop this intimacy with God, is the same way you did with your spouse (if you're married) when you were dating (or any good friend as you seek to know each other more fully)...through time with Him. You can't get *drive-through* or *microwave* intimacy. It just doesn't happen that way. It takes intentional time with Him.

Affirmation for today: Today, I will choose to respond instead of react. I will exercise a sacred pause, and seek God before speaking.

Be quick to listen, slow to speak, and slow to become angry.

(James 1:19)

Here's a story, told by her mother, of a little girl who understands what it means to pray expectantly:

Years ago when my two girls were small, they were taught how to pray before eating their meal. One night as I was busy scurrying around the kitchen, I told them both to pray without me. I took a moment to watch them as they both squeezed their eyes tightly shut over folded hands. As my 4- year-old finished, her 3-year-old sister kept on praying. Another minute or two passed before she lifted her head, looked at her plate, and in an indignant voice said, "Hey! My peas are still here!"

Do you expect God to answer your prayers?

"When everything seems to be going against you, remember that the airplane takes off against the wind, not with it."

~Henry Ford

Are you choosing to think about what is good and praiseworthy rather than dwelling on the bad, worrisome stuff in your life?

"Worry gives a small thing a big shadow."
~Swedish Proverb

What are you making a big shadow of?

Father, You are so cool! Thank You for Your creation—there is so much good all around me! Help me focus on that goodness, on the positive stuff rather than my problems. I know that I will encounter trouble but I also know that the good stuff You have blessed me with is so much greater than my problems. Help me focus on the truly important things in my life. Especially help me to focus more on You so that You can reveal to me what is important to You. Amen.

"Every adversity, every failure and every heartache carries with it the seed of an equivalent or a greater benefit."

~Napoleon Hill

The plans of the diligent lead to profit as surely as haste leads to poverty.

(Proverbs 21:5)

Is there any planning you could do which would reduce the stress in your life?

"There are two ways to sleep well at night—be ignorant or be prepared."

~Simon Black

What do you need to do to get prepared?

Affirmation for today: I can trust God in all disagreements.

Disagreements are healthy.

How much margin do you have in your schedule?

If you were able to create some breathing room, how would that make you feel?

"The gem cannot be polished without friction, nor man perfected without trials."

~Chinese Proverb

God is the One who controls outcomes, but He also wants us to plan. God can obviously change our plans; however, our planning often gets us into the proper position.

Have you done any planning? How is that helping or hindering the level of peace you are presently experiencing?

Lord, You are a God of order and I am thankful for that. Lord, I want more order in my life. Please guide me and give me the self-control to take the time to plan with You, even if I don't want to. Help me see the incredible benefits that can come from this. Help me acknowledge You in all my ways so You can make my paths straight. Thank You Lord! Amen.

Affirmation for today: I will take my feelings to God and share with others I trust.

Therefore confess your sins to each other and pray for each other so that you may be healed.
(James 5:16a)

"I have told you these things, so that in me you may have peace."
(The words of Jesus in John 16:33a)

Did you know that in Jesus you may have peace? Ponder that today.

Whatever you have learned or received or heard from me, or seen in me—put it into practice. And the God of peace will be with you.

(Philippians 4:9)

Did you know that God is referred to as the "God of peace" more than any other adjective in the Bible?

"In three words I can sum up everything I've learned about life. *It goes on.*"

~Robert Frost

Affirmation for today: I am free to be who God made me to be and to live life to the full.

"The thief comes only to steal and kill and destroy; I have come that they may have life, and have it to the full."

(The words of Jesus in John 10:10)

We were made to do life in community.

Who is your community? Who could you ask to fill that role?

Have you ever heard it said that the safest place to be is in God's will? That's not true. It is the *best* place, but most would agree it is not the *safest* place. Look at Peter. The safest place for him would have been to remain in the boat. He chose the riskier of the options and saw a miracle when he stepped out onto the water because that's where Jesus was.

"The difference between stumbling blocks and stepping stones is how you use them."

~Unknown

"I have told you these things, so that in me you may have peace. In this world you will have trouble. **But** take heart! I have overcome the world"

> (The words of Jesus in John 16:33, emphasis added).

Ponder the truth of this today:
1. In Jesus you may have peace
2. You cannot escape trouble...it is a part of life
3. **But** take heart! Jesus has overcome the world...including your troubles.

Note: Jesus said he *has* already overcome the world...it is done!

"But seek first his kingdom and his righteousness, and all these things will be given to you as well." (The words of Jesus in Matthew 6:33)

How can you seek first God's kingdom and His righteousness today?

Following Jesus is not the path to an easy life, yet Jesus is the only way to true, God-given peace. He is the most important piece—He is the beginning and the end.

Father, You are beyond words. I love You so much and I thank You for loving me like You do. I thank You for providing a way to peace. I can see that Jesus is the only way to find that peace, the peace, which surpasses all understanding. And Lord, that's what I want...that's what I am seeking right now. Please forgive me for the times that I have stayed in my comfort zone. Help me, and even challenge me, to break out of that place that I think is safe. Help me to see that it is only outside of my comfort zone where Jesus is. Help me to be like Peter and step out of the boat into the arms of Jesus so I can take hold of the peace, which He has brought me. Finally God, help me to imprint Your words on my heart so that I can have Your peace in me the rest of my days. Amen.

Would you like some resources to help you go deeper in your quest for peace?

Go to 5feet20.com to find many things that can help you, including:

Jim's other books, including...

- *Calming the Storm Within: How to Find Peace in this Chaotic World* (printed, ebook and audio)
- *Calming the Storm Within Workbook*
- *Bleedership: Biblical First-Aid for Leaders - Expanded Edition* (printed, ebook and audio)

Jim's Retreat Kit (very helpful for intentional times away with God)

Jim's Peace Insider Roundtable coaching group

Five Feet Twenty free monthly magazine, a quick read which will encourage you greatly

In addition, here is a link to receive Jim's free report, *The #1 Reason You are Filled with Stress & Anxiety and How to Keep Your Peace From Being Stolen* : 5feet20.com/free-report-more-peace/